TRAILBLAZING TEAMS
GROUPS OF PEOPLE WHO HAVE CHANGED THE WORLD

THE HUMAN COMPUTERS

WRITTEN BY
EMILIE DUFRESNE

DESIGNED BY
DANIELLE RIPPENGILL

BookLife PUBLISHING

ISBN: 978-1-83927-692-7

©2021
**BookLife Publishing Ltd.
King's Lynn
Norfolk PE30 4LS**

Written by:
Emilie Dufresne

Edited by:
Madeline Tyler

Designed by:
Danielle Rippengill

All facts, statistics, web addresses and URLs in this book were verified as valid and accurate at time of writing. No responsibility for any changes to external websites or references can be accepted by either the author or publisher.

CONTENTS

Words that look like this can be found in the glossary on page 24.

VAUGHAN

I changed what I could, and what I couldn't, I endured.

Who was Dorothy Vaughan?

How did she help other Black women in <u>NASA</u>?

MARY JACKSON

Who was Mary Jackson?

How did she become NASA's first Black female engineer?

'She was a scientist, humanitarian, wife, mother, and trailblazer who paved the way for thousands of others to succeed, not only at NASA, but throughout this nation.'

- Carolyn Lewis, Mary's daughter

JACKSON

KATHERINE JOHNSON

Everything was so new – the whole idea of going into space was new and daring. There were no textbooks, so we had to write them.

JOHNSON

Who was Katherine Johnson?

How did she help humans to land on the Moon?

THE WOMEN BEHIND THE WORKINGS

DOROTHY VAUGHAN

Dorothy Vaughan was born in 1910 in the US.

She got a **degree** in maths and went on to be a maths teacher. In 1943, she began working as a human computer at NACA, which would later become NASA.

DOROTHY VAUGHAN

MARY JACKSON

Mary Jackson was born in the US in 1921.

She went to **university** and got a degree in maths and science. She worked in lots of different jobs before working in Dorothy's team at NACA.

MARY JACKSON

KATHERINE JOHNSON

Katherine Johnson was born in 1918 in the US.

She was very clever from a young age and earned a degree in maths and French at the age of 18, three years earlier than most. In 1953, she started working at NACA.

LEARN MORE ABOUT HUMAN COMPUTERS ON PAGE 10.

KATHERINE JOHNSON

MAKING IT IN MATHS

THESE PEOPLE WERE CALLED THE HUMAN COMPUTERS.

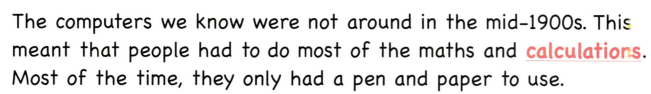

The computers we know were not around in the mid-1900s. This meant that people had to do most of the maths and **calculations**. Most of the time, they only had a pen and paper to use.

During **World War Two**, many men were sent away to fight. This meant lots of women had the chance to become human computers. They often had to do maths to help male engineers.

BEING SEGREGATED

When Dorothy, Mary and Katherine joined NACA, there were different areas for white and Black people to work, eat and even go to the toilet. This was because of **segregation** in the US at the time.

These three women, and many others, were **discriminated** against for being both female and Black. They had to put up with many problems while working at NACA, but they never gave up or stopped working hard.

When NACA became NASA, it ended segregation.

MORE THAN A COMPUTER

Dorothy, Mary and Katherine faced a lot of discrimination while at work. However, they used their maths knowledge to do amazing things and prove that they were more than computers.

Dorothy Vaughan was one of the first Black female human computers. She worked in more and more important jobs and ended up leading the team of Black human computers, including Mary and Katherine.

This team did the maths for engineers who were <u>experimenting</u> on <u>aircraft.</u>

Mary Jackson went to **court** in order to go to a 'white only' school to get the **qualifications** she needed to become the first Black female engineer at NASA.

JACKSON

Katherine Johnson used her maths to work out the journeys spacecraft would take, and how to land them safely. Her maths even helped to land humans on the Moon!

LIFTING UP OTHERS

These women also did amazing things for other women and Black people.

Dorothy Vaughan became NACA's first Black female team leader. As team leader, she made sure the women who worked for her got the jobs and pay they deserved.

VAUGHAN

Mary Jackson was a successful engineer and went on to help women and other discriminated groups go further in science, engineering and maths. She made sure they knew what they could achieve and how to do it.

MARY JACKSON

LEAVING A LEGACY

In 2015, Katherine Johnson was awarded the Presidential Medal of Freedom by Barack Obama for her work as a Black woman in science.

KATHERINE JOHNSON

JOHNSON

DOROTHY VAUGHAN

Dorothy, Mary and Katherine achieved great things for science, Black people and women. They created pathways for the Black women who followed them, helping them to achieve even more.

They also proved that no matter what others think of you, you can achieve anything you put your mind to.

MARY JACKSON

A TRAILBLAZING TIMELINE

1910
DOROTHY VAUGHAN IS BORN

1918
KATHERINE JOHNSON IS BORN

1921
MARY JACKSON IS BORN

1951
MARY JACKSON AND KATHERINE JOHNSON JOIN NACA

1943
DOROTHY VAUGHAN JOINS NACA

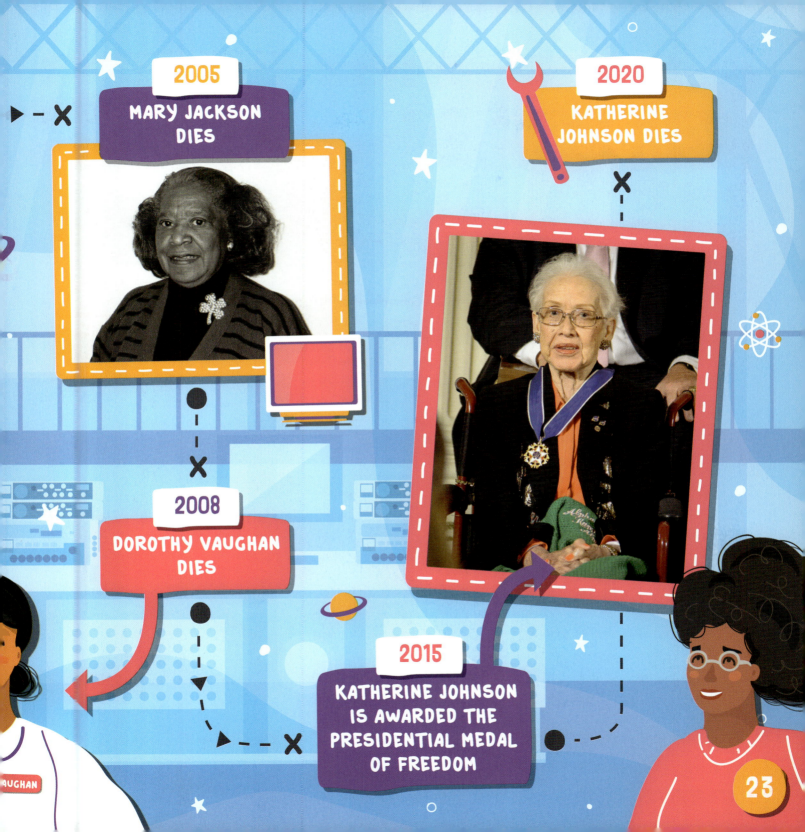

2005

MARY JACKSON DIES

2020

KATHERINE JOHNSON DIES

2008

DOROTHY VAUGHAN DIES

2015

KATHERINE JOHNSON IS AWARDED THE PRESIDENTIAL MEDAL OF FREEDOM

VAUGHAN

23

GLOSSARY

aircraft — any vehicle that can fly, for example aeroplanes and helicopters

calculations — the workings out of maths

court — a place where a judge can make decisions about the law

degree — a level of education that you are often awarded with after going to university

discriminated — to have been unfairly treated differently to someone else because of things such as the colour of your skin, your age or your religion

engineer — a person who designs and builds complex things such as machines

experimenting — doing tests to try and find something out

NASA — National Aeronautics and Space Administration, the space agency in the US

qualifications — special skills or knowledge that you train or study to complete and get a certificate for

segregation — separating groups of people based on the untrue belief that some people aren't as good as others because of things such as the colour of their skin

university — a place where people go to study, usually after they are 18

World War Two — a war that took place between the years of 1939 and 1945

INDEX